newborn life

FOSTERING **JOY** IN THE FIRST YEAR OF MOTHERHOOD

Front cover illustration: LeonART/Shutterstock.com | Back cover illustration: xgw1028/Shutterstock.com | Dedication page flourish: Megin/Shutterstock.com
Written by Anne Peace and Christine Desforges
Design and layout by Christine Desforges
Copy edited by Linda Stulberg

For information, please contact: newbornlifebook@gmail.com

First edition
Published and printed in Canada

Library and Archives Canada Cataloguing in Publication

Peace, Anne
    Newborn life : fostering joy in the first year of motherhood / Anne Peace, Christine Desforges.

ISBN 978-1-926863-54-2

    1. Motherhood--Psychological aspects.
2. Parenting--Psychological aspects.
3. Happiness. I. Desforges, Christine II. Title.

HQ759.P425 2012   306.874'3   C2011-908619-0

Library and Archives Canada registration
and production management
through the TRI Publishing™ program
TRIMATRIX Management Consulting Inc.
www.trimatrixmanagement.com

{ *Dedications* }

To my mum Bee and dad Cap, who gave me life and love: thank you.

To my twin sister Lizzie, my brother John, and all my stunning friends
who have helped me grow in life and in love: thank you.

To my son Lee and my daughter Emma,
to whom I gave life and love: thank you.

To my daughter-in-law Jenny, my granddaughter Veronica Grace,
and all the new souls who join us in this legacy of life and love:
thank you.

– Anne

To my mom Linda, who brought me into this world,

My sister Laura, who let me stay.

My daughter Jaclyn, who made it all make sense.

And my son-in-law Dan: welcome to the family.

Heart = full.

– Chris

{ *Acknowledgements* }

We are grateful to family and friends who have forever inspired and encouraged us. Thank you.

We also wish to thank Sheryl Lubbock and her team at Trimatrix Management Consulting Inc., whose expertise made this book a reality.

Our book has been enriched by personal stories submitted by our contributors – Jenny Gilbert, Eva Martinez, Claire Plivcic, Pat Roberts, Jill Snidal and Elizabeth Wickerman. We thank each of you for sharing your lives with other mothers everywhere.

And for the invaluable feedback from those who read our manuscript as we progressed, we offer our thanks to Jaclyn Desforges, Jenny Gilbert, Linda Leonard, Lee Sheppard, Jill Snidal, Jamie Sutherland and Janet Sutherland.

To copy editor Linda Stulberg, whose know-how allows us to sleep at night. Thank you for all your pencilled notes and the thoughtful skill behind them.

To all the mothers from Anne's Find Your Joy group: this book would never have been born without your warmth, wisdom, strength and honesty. We are forever humbled.

Contents

This book was written for new mothers who are navigating their way through the first year of parenthood. Here, we acknowledge the life changes a new mother might experience and the range of emotions that can be part of this journey. We also offer some ideas on how to make the trip more joyful.

This book is not intended to take the place of professional assistance. If you or someone you know suffers from postpartum depression or any other serious physical or emotional problems please seek help immediately from a qualified professional.

Although this is a book for mothers by mothers, we heartfully acknowledge that fathers also play a vital role in the healthy development of families and children. We hope that everyone who cares for babies – including parents, other family members and trusted friends – finds value in our message.

A word about pronouns: Rather than using a gender-neutral "s/he" or something similar, we have opted to alternate between male and female pronouns throughout the text of this book.

Introduction Christine Desforges

On a blustery February morning in 1989, I pushed through the heavy doors of the Toronto Women's Bookstore. The cold wind blew straight through the winter coat that I couldn't zip. Baby weight. I inadvertently dragged snow inside from the sidewalk – I could hardly lift my feet. Exhaustion. I had not slept more than three hours in a row for 50 days. And it would be another 50 nights before I did.

I felt fat and I was tired. But I was on a mission. I was looking for a book – the book that would help me make sense of my life as a new mom.

I so desperately needed this book that I left my breastfed seven-week-old baby girl with a bottle of formula (and her grandmother) to drive 40 snow-covered miles to find it. It was my 26th birthday, and I had been reborn into a body and a life I didn't recognize. In my post-partum haze, I thought a bookstore for women might hold some answers.

I wanted to know what was wrong with me. I needed to know why being a mother didn't feel the way I expected it to feel. I felt confident taking care of Jaclyn, but inside I was scattered and off-balance. Where was the calm and the joy I saw on the faces of the moms in all the magazines? And if my struggles were normal, why hadn't anyone told me what to expect?

In spite of my efforts, I didn't find what I needed that day, or any other day. I couldn't even ask. Back then, I didn't know how to describe what I needed. At any rate, the book hadn't yet been written. It didn't exist in 1989 because it is the book you are holding in your hands.

And you are reading it now only because of my friend Anne Peace. She opened the conversation by creating a workshop called Find Your Joy at the Parent-Child Centre in Oakville, Ont. In that class, Anne has made a safe place for young moms to express themselves, realize they are not alone, and gain some powerful information about what they can do for themselves to create more happiness in their lives. Once a week, young mothers stop, take a breath and have a chance to look within themselves for the answers they seek.

Anne has filled a very real need. Apparently, I wasn't alone in my confusion more than 20 years ago. Although there are a lot more sources of information and connection now than there were back then, new moms everywhere still struggle to find the wisdom they need to become the mothers they strive to be.

So together Anne and I decided to write this book about what it is to be a new mother. As she does in her class, we discuss the realities and paradoxes of early parenting. We ask important questions about ourselves as people and as parents. Then we present information about positive psychology – an exciting new science still in its own infancy. We hope that all of this together gives you valuable insights and useful tools as you begin your journey into motherhood.

Most of all, we want you to feel the support and encouragement we believe every new mother deserves. If we can help you get up tomorrow morning with a lighter heart, a better understanding of yourself, and greater confidence in the important work you are doing in your first year of motherhood, then we have done our job. You will know it, your baby will feel it – and you will find more happiness together in this newborn life you share. – CD

Introduction Anne Peace

When Chris showed me what she had written as an introduction to this book, I was deeply moved. Her words touched my heart and reached down to my core. I got goose bumps. I had been on a search in those bookstores too.

In 1972, I graduated from the University of Toronto with a Bachelor of Science in Nursing. I worked as a public health nurse for three years in the Region of Peel and then left to go to Sheridan College in Oakville, Ont., to become an early childhood educator. I was married to a family doctor. (Can you see the white picket fence?) It was the summer after I graduated from Sheridan that I gave birth to my first child, a son named Lee.

What a shock. Foolishly, I thought that with all my credentials I would handle the role of new mother with expertise. To make matters worse, I was a perfectionist. And my very entrenched perfectionism had a destructive life all its own.

I was a mess. I needed help and I needed to lighten up. And I wanted to know where all the happiness went – the joy that I felt sure would come from simply holding my newborn baby.

I didn't know where to turn. I felt shame that we didn't look like the mothers and babies in the books that I saw. The mothers looked beautiful and the babies did too. Me? I looked and felt more tired than I ever had in my life. Breastfeeding caused me pain. My episiotomy was not healing well. Simply using the bathroom introduced me to a whole new world of suffering. It felt as if my body didn't belong to me anymore. (I was right – it didn't.)

Let's face it, I was scared and vulnerable. How on Earth was I going to manage being a mother? But no one knew how I struggled because I went into hiding with my feelings.

I remember the moment when I "came out." Lee was about four months old. It was late in the afternoon, and we had experienced a difficult day of crying (both of us). Colic and confusion were putting us on a path to catastrophe. I knew that I needed to put Lee down. I felt helpless and ineffective – I was the mother who couldn't even comfort her own child.

As I rounded the corner of his bedroom, I hit his head on the door frame. I can still see it in slow motion – for that is the moment when perfect Anne realized that if she didn't get some help, her baby might be harmed. I don't think I have ever cried so hard or felt my humanity as deeply.

After that day, I began to reach out. I arranged time for myself each week and found the courage to talk to friends. Accident or not, it didn't matter. What mattered was that I scrapped the unrealistic expectations that were making my life so very miserable, and found a new and more realistic approach to mothering my son.

Becoming a mother is a journey of discovery. The way you are as a mother will be different from the way that I am a mother. Give yourself the space to go slowly and imperfectly to the home of your mother's heart. This book wants to help. It wants to tell a story and encourage you to tell your story.

This book also shares the principles of a wonderful research base of knowledge called positive psychology. Infused throughout are thoughts on how to use the principles of positive psychology to help you thrive as a mother and as a family.

There is joy in this job. We want to help you find it. – AP

Our Intention

Throughout this book, we offer ideas to help you experience more happiness during your first year as a parent. Our hope is to be the calming voice that comforts you in the midst of this challenging time.

We believe that each new mom needs to be reminded of her strengths in the face of the noise and confusion and well-meaning advice that can muffle her instincts and her belief in herself as a capable parent. We also believe it is profoundly reassuring to know that you are not alone (and not crazy) as you navigate the challenges of your child's first year.

We want to assure you that you are perfectly capable of becoming the mother you want to be. As you learn to nurture your child, and as you begin to trust your own skill and judgment, we intend to validate your experience and encourage you at every turn. Within these pages, we share our hard-won wisdom to help you find yourself – and lay the foundation for some solid parenting.

But we cannot tell you exactly what your family's life will look like, nor will we offer a "one size fits all" framework to follow. Our wisdom tells us that it's not the coming to the "right" decision (cloth or disposable, schedule or demand, blanket or sweater) that makes a good parent; rather it's the fact that you care enough to struggle with all the options available to you, and that you strive to make your life authentically your own.

To that end, we encourage you to rely on your inner self: your intuition. It's a most valuable resource. Tapping into your core knowledge helps you trust yourself. Only then will you settle into the happiness that can become the foundation of your new life.

We want you to create the beginnings of a well-lived life for your family. We humbly and respectfully offer our very best, and encourage you to use the ideas that are most helpful to you. Here, as in life, feel free to disregard the rest.

Part 1: Two New Lives

What you might not know is that there are really two new lives: your child's and your own. You may think that your baby will slip neatly into the life you already have. What you don't realize is that you will be completely transformed by this thing called motherhood.

9

Love has arrived...

Congratulations.
You did it.

It's a BABY!
You have created a human being.
A miracle.

As much as you just had a baby,
that baby just had you too.

As this new life begins, your life
will change forever.

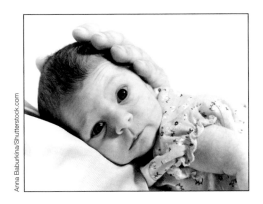

It's hard to believe. Your baby is finally here, and you have given her a wonderful start. Healthy and anything but helpless, she commands attention with every tiny squeak. If that doesn't work, she already knows how to dial up the volume to let everyone know what she needs, and when she needs it. It doesn't hurt that she is the cutest baby ever, and she just about glows with all that is fresh and new.

You, on the other hand, may not be feeling as bright or shiny. Many new moms are surprised at how bruised and bewildered they feel after the birth of a child. Healing can take longer than you think – weeks, not days – and much longer than our culture acknowledges. At the same time, you have a life completely changed and a newborn to nurture. And caring for that baby can be exhausting.

You will be amazed at the sheer hard work such a tiny person requires. It's not that the tasks are particularly difficult, it's the amount of time they take. You can expect to feed her up to 12 times in 24 hours (each one 45 minutes or longer) and do a dozen diaper changes each day. Add in cleaning, comforting and respond-ing as needed – don't even try to do the math in your postpartum head – and you quickly run out of hours in the day. (And, of course, every-thing takes twice as long as you think.)

But it's no accident that Mother Nature keeps you so very busy and never lets you forget what you have created. These round-the-clock tasks not only keep the baby warm, fed and clean, they teach an intricate dance of care and connection. You are laying the foundation for your life as a family and becoming an elbows-deep mother.

True, nurturing a newborn is all-consuming – maybe the most exhausting work you will ever take on. But it all adds up to much more than fresh bums and drowsy burps – this is a critical time for bonding and love, and it is perhaps the most important work of your entire life.

How can such relatively easy tasks become the hardest of work? Perhaps the most critical work of our entire lives…

You can do this – really!

When you invite new life in, life happens. All of life: the dull stretches and the sad bits and the moments of pure joy. And then there are the times when you look at your precious child and ask yourself what you have done – to yourself, to your partner, and to your life as you once knew it.

The truth is that any life change, even a positive one, can bring grief, fear and stress as you close one chapter and begin the next. Becoming a parent offers a unique opportunity to feel the full spectrum of emotions. Some parts will feel exhilarating. Other times, in a sea of diapers and a wave of colic, you may feel over-whelmed. Mothering can also be incredibly tedious. The challenge comes when you feel all those feelings in the same afternoon, or in the same 30 seconds.

This transition to motherhood is a big one because there are so many things going on. Not only are you healing physically from carrying and birthing a child, you have whole lot of new things happening in your life and in your home. There is no gradual transition – it's all day every day, and all night long as well, right from day one.

A new role, a new baby, a new round-the-clock schedule, all at once. It's not neat and tidy – the familiar is gone and it's easy to feel confused. And having any time or energy to sort through your emotions is one of the luxuries that gets crowded out when the baby arrives.

This is why becoming a parent is one of the biggest life-changers on this Earth. Feeling adrift – or any other emotion for that matter – is completely normal. You will not escape unchanged. In fact, you will never be the same. Not. Ever. Again.

But here's the good news: you can be better than you ever were. You will live a richer existence and feel more joy than you ever imagined. We promise that this journey will prove to be well worth it.

But – and this is the part people most often get wrong – having a baby, in itself, will not make you happy. What you get are the precious raw materials – the purpose and light and colour and awesome responsibility – that make you a parent. The joy comes only when you let those things transform your world and change every last thing you thought you ever knew.

You may not be able to tell a friend everything she might experience as a mom, but you can answer her questions about what mothering is like for you.

When we share what it true for us, we fortify our deepest selves and invite real joy to enter our lives.

But why didn't anybody tell me?

No one told you because, simply put, many of life's bigger truths have to be lived to be learned. And life has its own way of teaching its lessons to every new mother.

You really can't blame the people around you for not sharing all the details up front. Anyone with child-rearing experience knows that when it comes to babies, nothing is certain and no one can say for sure. You are living your own story – who could possibly predict your birth experience or tell you how it will all play out? Except to say that life with any newborn is never easy. And to expect to slide into this momentous role without any kind of adjustment is unrealistic. To struggle is normal.

Just as your struggles are unique, so are your gifts. You have to find them for yourself, then figure out how to open them. But it's tricky. In this realm, paradox doubles as gift wrap – at first glance, some of your blessings won't look like gifts at all. For instance, in those three o'clock feedings, you might feel a strength and sense of purpose like never before. In motherhood's

monotony, you may find your creativity. In its solitude, you have a rich opportunity to discover yourself. This could be the biggest gift of all. If you give it a chance, make the space and meet the challenges, you might just become the best of who you were meant to be. But it isn't easy. It is many things, but it's never easy.

But the biggest reason nobody told you is simple: it's all too hard to explain. There's so much more to the story – more than anyone can ever express. Like how incredibly fascinating and mind-numbing parenting can be, all at the same time. Or the depth of unconditional love you are feeling for the very first time. Or what it's like to be willing to step in front of a speeding train to save this tiny child. And how strangely normal it feels to be imagining (and fearing) life-and-death scenarios in the middle of the night.

No one told you because this is a story only you can tell for yourself. It is all too big for words. It's awesome, this mothering thing, even when it's not. And there's no explaining any of that.

Now breathe.

Take a moment, take a breath.
Breathe deeply, as deeply as you can.
Now exhale.

There, that's better.

Before we move on...
a word about sleep

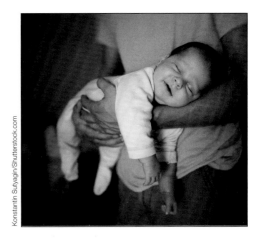

Konstantin Sutyagin/Shutterstock.com

Sleep deprivation is a very big deal. It takes 14 days or more to starve from lack of food, but just 10 days without sleep can kill you.

Conversely, you can live without folded socks and dusted furniture for much longer – forever, in fact.

Every child-care manual tells you to sleep when the baby sleeps, and for good reason. Sleep deprivation is used as torture in some parts of the world. Anyone who has experienced chronic lack of sleep will tell you exactly how torturous it can be.

Yet losing sleep can seem like some kind of badge of honour that every new parent earns. In a world where naps are for wimps, getting proper rest can feel like a feeble thing to do. And even if you do love a satisfying snooze, the 42 minutes of personal freedom that come when baby sleeps can seem far too seductive to waste on unconsciousness.

Still, you need to value rest and make your sleep a priority, especially in the early weeks. If not for yourself, do it for your newborn. Proper rest will help you heal faster and care for your baby better. If need be, other people can help with chores, but no one can sleep for you. Or, for that matter, breathe or eat or drink for you – so be gentle and kind and take care of yourself in every way.

Signs of sleep deficit:

- It's dinner time and you're pretty sure you never had lunch.

- You've started folding laundry and writing a thank you note and checking the email – all in the last three minutes.

- You forget where you put the diaper bag. And what your diaper bag looks like.

- Conversation? What were we talking about again?

- Taking a little nap on the steering wheel seems like a reasonable option.

- You feel achy and kind of sick all over.

Saying goodbye to the old

Once your child is born, you know what it is to truly put someone else first. You know what it is to love unconditionally. It's a humbling, deeply moving experience that separates parents from everyone else. It matures us, and it's so very worth the trouble.

Still, the round-the-clock nature of caring for a newborn can frazzle even the most grounded, prepared and committed new parent. The deep shift at the very centre of our being and newfound focus invariably sends ripples throughout every part of our lives. Don't be alarmed if your ripples start to feel like waves, or even small tsunamis. When you have been accustomed to planning your own day, doing things with both hands, and receiving regular rewards for your good work, there can be a feeling of loss when you become totally responsible for another life seven days a week, 24 hours a day.

True, parenting is supposed to be selfless, but it's perfectly acceptable for you to mourn the loss of your former life and your freedom. In fact, it's more than acceptable: to enjoy a healthy life, processing the feelings that come with transitions is a requirement.

Maridav/Shutterstock.com

And welcoming the new

Of course, there is no denying that your life has fundamentally changed. Still, people try to maintain their before-the-baby lives without skipping a beat. But starting from the very first moment on the very first day, it becomes joyfully clear that it's truly not all about you anymore.

The baby comes first, even if you're tired or sick and even if it's your birthday. And if you forget, he will remind you, loudly and clearly. This has been the way of things since the beginning of time. You can try, but your best intentions and most carefully made plans are not going to change this life shift.

Yes, it can be scary to let go of the old life before you can clearly see the new one and how it will play out. Don't worry – it's there. Lean on in. You will not find any of this bottomless. The act of surrender – and truly putting your child's needs ahead of your own – will only serve to empower you for everything that lies ahead.

It helps to look ahead with a sense of wonder and curiosity. Only then will you be able to say goodbye to your life as it was, and look forward to the rewards that can now be yours.

You will feel it happen. Early on, right after you fall in love with him, you will notice a place of strength growing at the centre of your being. Each day afterward, as you embrace the ups and downs and frustrations and joys of your new life, that strength grows. This is just the beginning of you becoming the mom you were meant to be.

But you have to find your own way to the gifts of motherhood, and for each of us the rewards will be different. You might grow the backbone you've always needed, or become less rigid and more compassionate. However it goes, you will realize that everything you need is already inside you, ready to be revealed. And all the qualities that make you such a wonderful mother are also making you a much better human being.

You have been reborn as a mom, and you are brand new too. Welcome.

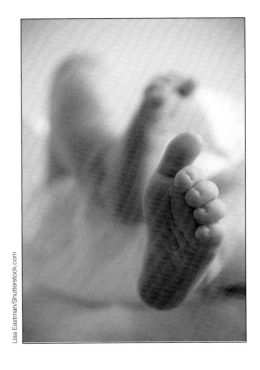

Lisa Eastman/Shutterstock.com

Let this new relationship with this new little person work on you – break you maybe, then teach you. And it will, but only if you let it.

Connection, not perfection

Make the connection and there can be love in that basket of half-done laundry.

We were taught to work for the outcome we wanted – to push forward for that good grade, promotion or a new job. We made lists, set goals and completed tasks. And hard work brought success. Perhaps we even got a little hooked on the thrill of achievement and the illusion of control over the things that were happening in our lives.

The thing is, motherhood isn't like that, especially when you are mothering an infant. You can work yourself silly all day long (and night) and have nothing to show for it except a smiling baby. Or in the first weeks, not even a smile – just the baby.

Know that new mothers everywhere stumble through their child's first days, caught up in this new role where there is no control over what happens when, with no recognizable reward for weeks on end. Schedules get thrown off course and to-do lists go unchecked when you have a newborn who needs your care and comfort. Familiar coping methods simply don't work. And that's completely normal because, unlike your old life, this new way of living is all about connection, not perfection.

It's about connection with your baby and connection to your experience as a new mother. There is a happy side effect. Here is your chance to start to give up trying to be perfect and become a more authentic version of yourself in a life that doesn't always sparkle. And maybe you will settle back into the self you might have lost before everything became so fast-paced and ruled by outside pressures, agendas and expectations.

Here is a wonderful opportunity to connect to the rhythms of your baby's pace and focus on her needs. Don't miss the chance to learn to accept where you are and what is happening in the now, and to feel it all as it unfolds. Because once the dust settles, happiness comes when you can truly live in the moment.

And now that life has changed, you can see how on some days, simply getting to through it all in one piece is the greatest success you can achieve.

Besides, it is all perfect just as it is, even if it looks like a mess by your old life's standards. Because in all this chaos lies your opportunity to make some joy.

Now is not the time to take up the tuba...

Often, new moms make plans to complete projects during their time away from the paid workplace after they have their baby – things like painting the living room or learning Spanish. It's no wonder: our society encourages constant productivity. We feel good when we have something to show for ourselves and we feel badly when we don't – and the faster the better. Breakneck speed is the accepted pace, not only for ourselves but for everyone else as well.

But such standards can't be applied to mothering. If you try, life quickly becomes a constant struggle of conflicting priorities. Instead, expect to feel a very real disconnect between your life and the lives of everyone else

you know. Save yourself unnecessary distress by accepting the fact that that you can't complete any kind of project when it's impossible to even finish a cup of coffee.

It's not your fault. Having a baby and caring for that baby has a pace all its own. Mothering is a primitive act – if you let it, the experience will take you to who you are as a human being. Let yourself slow down and connect with the part of you who knows how to be and what to do.

And forget about the tuba for now. Making a new and joyful life after creating, birthing and nurturing a tiny person (and yourself) is enough achievement for this year – and maybe for next year too.

This year, it's all about making choices that support your peace of mind.

19

You are so much more

than you can even imagine.

And you deserve so much more happiness than you ever thought possible.

What is this thing called joy?

If happiness ranges from a feeling of mild contentment to waves of intense bliss, joy sits at the top of the scale. It's that vivid moment or hour or day when it all feels right and complete and we are bursting with everything positive that life on this Earth offers. We've all felt it, and every one of us could use more of it. The happier we are, the better our lives become. Our relationships become more satisfying and we are more likely to appreciate our blessings from a place of contentment. The good news is that joy is not as elusive we might believe.

We want to help you get closer to your joy, more often. We want you to feel the joy in mothering, or at the very least solid contentment and peace of mind that can become the foundation for your new family life. Because at our happiest, we find a path to who we really are – and joy can also lead us in becoming the kind of mother we want to be.

Now for the paradox: we can't be happy all the time. Nor can we act from a place of insightful calm all day, every day. We all get angry, hurt, confused, frustrated, depressed (to name just a few). Not only are these emotions often appropriate, it's really quite easy to be pulled toward the dark side on any given day, faster than most of us would care to admit.

The good news is that we need all these emotions. In order to know true joy, you need to feel the full rainbow of feelings. Intensity counts. And the broader your range of emotions, the greater your capacity for joy.

Besides embracing our emotions, recent scientific research by Martin Seligman has shown that there are practical things we can do to increase our happiness. The relatively new science of positive psychology tells us that we can actually change our brains to make our lives feel richer and more satisfying. There are tools we can use to build a happier life.

This is all good news. We don't have to wait until the baby sleeps, the bikini fits, or the lottery gods smile upon us to be happy. We do not even need to repaint. We can start now, today, from exactly where we are in our lives.

And truly, there is no better time than the first year of your child's life. There will never be a better time to stop and take a deep breath. This is a profound time of growth for both you and your baby. Laying the foundation now for greater happiness sets the stage for making the family life that you want to have, and developing the qualities in yourself that you'd like your child to see and emulate.

Part 2: Foster Your Joy

Photo courtesy of Anne Peace

We don't have to wait until the baby sleeps, the bikini fits, or the lottery gods smile upon us to be happy. We do not even have to repaint. We can start now, today, from exactly where we are in our lives.

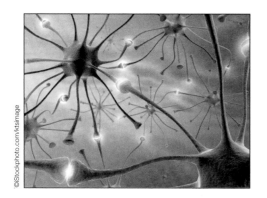

Positive psychology was officially launched by its founder, Martin Seligman, in 1998.

Research suggests that people who have increased their set point of happiness are able to recover more quickly and easily when life gets difficult.

Science and happiness – you can rewire your brain!

Even though it's a challenge, it is possible to change your brain on a neuronal level. We are capable of forming new pathways in our brains, even as adults. This is called neuroplasticity. Until the last decade or so, scientists weren't even sure it was possible in the adult brain. But it is. This is how it works:

The brain has neural pathways. Think of them as rivers and streams. Those pathways that are used a great deal are wider than those that are not used as much. When you learn a new skill, your pathway for that skill becomes thicker. And that is how habits form – fortified neural pathways. The more you focus on something or think about it, the more it becomes a habit. For example, when you first learned to drive, you felt very awkward behind the wheel. Now, after years of practice, driving has become a well-honed skill, and the vehicle feels like an extension of yourself.

It is the same for positive emotions. If you focus on the good, those pathways grow and thicken. The same applies to negative feelings. For example, when you worry a great deal, you make that "worry river" of the brain thicker. You can make worrying a habit.

You can break that habit – and many others – by rewiring your brain. How? You can start by deciding to make positivity a priority and focusing on the good. Then you can make use of the suggestions included in the following pages of this book. Try the things that feel right for you. You might be surprised at how you can learn to better cope with whatever life has to offer during this awesome, yet challenging time. You may even create more happiness and peace of mind for yourself.

But when it comes to your happiness, go slowly and expect the unexpected. Science tells us that human beings are not very good at predicting how much happiness we will experience in specific scenarios, or how long the feeling will last. So it makes perfect sense if you feel differently as a new mom than you thought you might feel.

Still, there are things you can do now to increase your potential joy and lay some solid groundwork for your future. If you want a happier life for yourself and your family, read on.

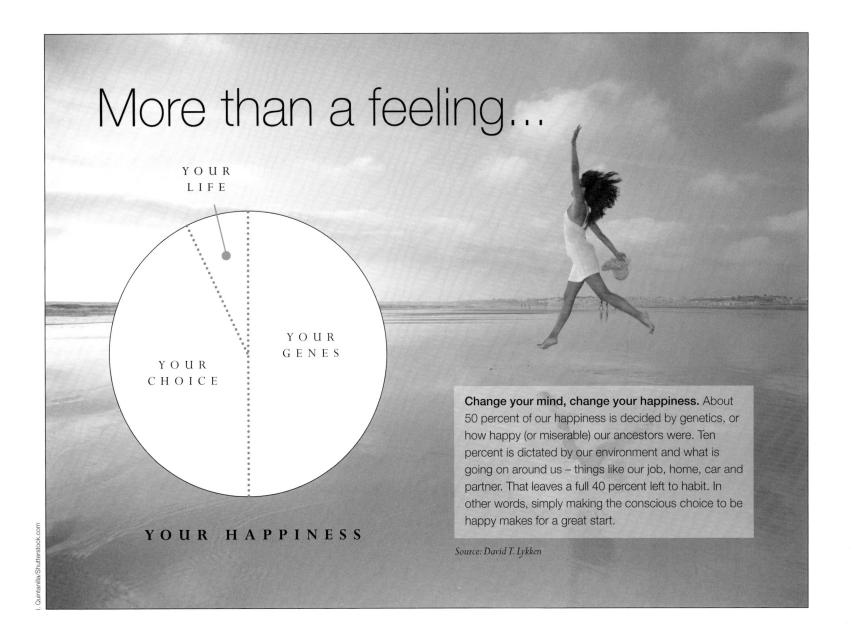

More than a feeling...

YOUR
LIFE

YOUR
CHOICE

YOUR
GENES

YOUR HAPPINESS

Change your mind, change your happiness. About 50 percent of our happiness is decided by genetics, or how happy (or miserable) our ancestors were. Ten percent is dictated by our environment and what is going on around us – things like our job, home, car and partner. That leaves a full 40 percent left to habit. In other words, simply making the conscious choice to be happy makes for a great start.

Source: David T. Lykken

Think happy.

We can choose to focus on fascination, love, hope, calm, patience and every other good thing in our lives.

We can feed our hearts and souls the things that exhilarate and captivate us.

Photograph by C. Desforges

Yes, you can learn to better cope with whatever life brings, acknowledge what goes right and create more happiness and peace of mind for yourself. But during this process, the science of positive psychology asks you to make changes. Before you shriek in protest and run for cover – we realize you've had lots of changes recently – please know that you are an ideal candidate. As a first-year parent, you're building a new life from the ground up. Why not incorporate some new habits that will bring you new happiness?

But please note that this will be a slow process that will move forward some days, stay the same or move backwards on other days. Happiness is a process, rather than a place. There is no final destination in this particular journey.

But you must promise to be loving and kind with yourself as you explore this new life. So let's start with self-compassion...

Practise self-compassion

Kindness for self that is devoid of judgment and evaluation

Sometimes we can become our own worst enemy. Our lives invariably involve all kinds of struggles and mistakes, and we tend to collapse into negativity any time we fail. But beating ourselves up doesn't make us better people, and it definitely doesn't make us better mothers. In fact, internal attacks like this can make us feel miserably inadequate and insecure about ourselves and our abilities.

On the other hand, if you learn to forgive yourself for your flaws and soothe your own hurts, you can embrace all of who you really are and become happier living in your own skin. When you believe you are a good person who deserves kindness, you will do good things for yourself and be more open to learning from life. You become free to take risks and win and lose and enjoy a very full journey.

And in mothering, if we are to teach the art of living to our children, a parent who practises self-compassion has much to offer. Imagine what it would mean to your child to see you learn from your struggles and take care of yourself in a kind way, then feel that same care coming his way when he loses, fails or feels the inevitable bumps and bruises of life.

Self-compassion involves active acceptance, a forgiving attitude and gentle self-talk. Start by thinking of a term of endearment that you can use to show support for yourself when you are having a tough time. The next time you feel upset, use the name to soothe and calm yourself.

By becoming your best friend, rather than your worst enemy, you can create a life all about learning and exploring, expressing rather than impressing. It will take practice, but the shift will be well worth it.

Jose AS Reyes/Shutterstock.com

Margaret M Stewart/Shutterstock.com

Cultivate the habit of gratitude

We all have plenty to be grateful for. When we focus on what's going right, we can learn to thrive like never before. Start by making a list of the gifts of motherhood as you have experienced them. Here are some ideas to get you started:

- Her nose nuzzled against your neck.
- Seeing what four o'clock in the morning looks like out your front window.
- You have the most compelling reason of all to get up each morning – and you no longer have to find your purpose in life.
- Strollers with cup holders.
- Sleepers with really big behinds.
- Newfound patience.
- Profound love that deepens every day.
- His gassy smiles.
- Playing... for the first time in a long time.
- Funny farts and tiny everything.

Science is telling us that a good portion of human happiness comes from creating meaning in our lives. We can do that by sharing love and kindness – and through gratitude.

Gratitude is about wanting what you have, not having what you want. When we express our gratitude, we attract abundance and even more reasons to be grateful.

Make it a daily ritual to cultivate gratitude in your life. Some people keep a gratitude journal where they list the things they are grateful for that day. Others give thanks every time they cross the threshold of their home. Do what feels right to you.

Showing gratitude toward the people in your life is another wonderful way to share love. Write a card or make extra food to share. You will both feel much better for it!

If you are new to gratitude, simply start with your breath. Close your eyes, inhale deeply and give thanks that you are living to enjoy yet another day in your awesome life adventure.

iofoto/Shutterstock.com

Joy is what happens when we allow ourselves to recognize how good things are – not necessarily how we want things to be, but just exactly as they are.

Live in the now

*…because now is where happiness lives
and there are blessings to be found
in the ordinary.*

Come home to yourself

The more you know about yourself, the better you will understand your desire to organize canned goods alphabetically and your need to own several label makers. Knowing more about your inner workings can clear away confusion and misconceptions and pave the way to better choices, which can lead to greater happiness.

You will have more compassion for yourself when you realize that you are sporting polka dots in a world (or playgroup) full of stripes. You will be happier when you can make decisions based upon your temperament because, without apology or second-guessing, you can steer clear of the things that don't suit you. Simply put, you can better embrace who you really are.

Temperament theory assigns you a colour or multi-letter designation through personality testing. You can also test for your signature strengths, and gauge just how satisfied you are with your life. Search online or read some of the resources that we recommend (see page 48). Or you can consult a life coach or other professional to guide you.

Want a great place to start? Pull out some old photos and check for clues in your own childhood. What did you like to do most? How did you spend your free time? What made you absolutely over-the-top happy?

"I'm really a BIRD? That explains SO MUCH about my life."

LenLis/Shutterstock.com

In a perfect world, what kind of mother would you be? What sort of mother will you really be?

Understanding yourself and increasing your knowledge of different personality styles and how they interact can also do wonders for your understanding of your child. Even the youngest of infants will reveal her unique self in the way she sleeps, eats, moves and interacts with the people and the world around her. As she grows, her temperament will become even more clearly defined.

But even if you and your child are alike, you will always be two separate souls, two separate reasons, two separate stories. Once you know this for sure, the discovery can begin. And true compassion can become the cornerstone for your life together.

Who are you? What do you need?
What do I need? And how will we connect?

Who are you, sweet child of mine?

Observe your feelings.

Observe your feelings as you would clouds passing in the sky. Notice how they come, notice how they go.

Notice how your feelings are not you.

Explore your emotions

It's not about ridding yourself of negative emotions – it's about exploring your feelings in the moment, so that you can deal with them without getting caught in a downward spiral of distress. It's an act of compassion and acceptance toward yourself, and a productive way to manage emotions like anger, jealousy, sadness, hurt and fear.

First, don't avoid, but connect. When a strong feeling arises, stop what you are doing and focus on how it feels in your body. Where are you feeling the physical sensation of the emotion? Is it a lump in your throat? Are there butterflies in your belly? Are you suddenly feeling waves of heat along your spine?

Listen to it. You might want to repress the feeling ("I'm not really angry") or project it onto the outer world ("Out of my way, Spot!"). Instead, make a space for the sensation that is coming up, breathe deeply and connect with the feeling as best you can.

Identify the emotion and stay with it. Name it, but don't get caught up in the story behind the feeling. Notice if you get distracted by imaginary conversations or scenarios playing out in your head. Breathe deeply and gently return your focus to the feeling in your body. If it helps, you can say some soothing words silently or aloud to calm yourself. After a few moments, the emotion may change to a different feeling or it may evaporate altogether.

This is a wonderful as a grounding exercise that can bring you back to your life in the here and now. The more you practise, the more comfortable you will become at sitting with yourself and your emotions, instead of fixating on the stories and the dramas that cause you unnecessary pain. This is a much better choice than focusing on the troublesome thoughts that can intensify the anguish you are feeling.

It can also be very empowering to know that, no matter what comes your way, you have the ability to manage your more challenging emotions and soothe yourself, by yourself.

You can learn to sit with your most challenging emotions, instead of letting them spiral into more pain than you really need to feel.

Reframe your life

We all have a well-worn list of big mistakes and embarrassing moments. But every time you remember how you fell down or screwed up or spit on your birthday cake as you blew out the candles, you have a choice. You can cringe and suffer all over again, or you can use the information in a meaningful way.

When you understand those bumps from a new perspective, you can begin to see them not only as inevitable in a well-lived life, but guideposts that helped you along the way. So thank goodness you got fired, because your next interview set you on a career path you were meant for – and a job that loves you back.

When you tell your life story, even to yourself, it helps to cast yourself as the hero who has overcome the odds, as opposed to the victim who has suffered to no end. We are not recommending ignoring pain, but only to begin to identify the lesson learned in all those moments you care not to repeat. And it doesn't hurt to notice how great you are for surviving and thriving in spite of all that adversity.

Loke Yek Mang/Shutterstock.com

Try to use reframing as you move forward as well. In your day-to-day life, reframing can improve the quality of your thinking. Start by paying attention to what you are pointing your mental camera at as you move through your day. Are you spending more time ruminating about the sink full of dirty dishes or celebrating with the baby who has just discovered his feet?

It works with emotions too. The key is to open up to the entire experience, rather than getting stuck in a narrow interpretation of the emotion caused by the situation. For instance, at a difficult moment, instead of jumping to think: "Anger is bad and I shouldn't feel angry," you can stop and become conscious of what is really going on. The thought can then become: "I feel angry because I'm tired and hungry. Now would be a great time to put the baby down and take a few moments to have a snack." Reframing removes the finger-wagging judgment, and clears the way to observing, accepting and acting productively to solve the problem.

It takes more effort to stay positive

…than it does to slide into the negative. It's normal to become engrossed in whatever isn't working in our lives.

Meditate

Meditation is a gift you give to yourself. You don't need to be a Buddhist monk to enjoy the rewards that meditation can bring. For busy moms, it can be a powerful tool for reducing stress and improving mood. Meditation encourages kindness and compassion, and can help you maintain a positive approach. It is also a time for you to relax and become more self-aware.

But for all its benefits, meditation does not have to be time-consuming or complicated. The key is to make it yours – the best form of meditation is the one that works best for you. You can meditate in a chair or on the floor, outside or in. Create a space, if you'd like – one with treasures that reflect and support who you are. You may want to look at a flickering candle or close your eyes. You may prefer early morning or late at night. It may be five minutes or 20, with music or a recorded guided session or in silence. Do what feels right to you.

The key is to keep your mind clear. When thoughts bubble up, nudge them aside gently, or just watch them come and go. Keep sitting and keep breathing. You are creating a place inside where feelings can surface and become neutral, where there is peace, comfort and retreat. Once you feel it, you will want to return again and again.

Luna Vandoorne/Shutterstock.com

If you want to learn about meditation, reach out to a group in your community. In the meantime, here is an exercise to try. **Mindful breathing can help you feel more relaxed and better able to enjoy whatever life brings.** Sit comfortably on a chair or on the floor. Take a deep breath. Feel the air as it enters the middle of your chest. Now exhale from deep inside, as if you are releasing stress that you have been holding within. Inhale and exhale mindfully at least four or five times. For best results, practise several times a day – each time you sit to feed your baby, for example.

Accentuate the positive

Keep the positive front and centre! You can make this project as simple as you need it to be. Use the fridge and magnets, or sticky notes and a blank wall, to display anything and everything that makes you smile. Write a list to remind yourself of your accomplishments. Make note of every compliment anyone has ever given you. Include cards you received when your baby came, photos, love notes, inspiring quotes – anything that reminds you of all the good things you have going on in your life. If you prefer, you can file it all in a special box, binder or scrap book. Make it a habit to regularly look through your collection.

Edit the messages you are absorbing – you may find you are more sensitive to what's going on in the world. If the TV news bothers you, don't watch it for a while. Fashion magazines are out when you are living in sweat pants. Beware of social media pages and the lives online that look so much better than your own. Remember that people never post the tedium, just the awesome. Read, see and hear the things that support you in the here and now. If it makes you miserable, turn it off or take it out.

Breathe in.

{Say "let."}

Breathe out.

{Say "go."}

Find community

Be brave enough to reach out when you feel lonely. Although solitude has its perks, we all need one another, and there are times when we are simply better together.

At the very least, a sense of community encourages fun. Other mothers will remind you to laugh and make time for the things that make you happy. As you get to know each other, you and your companions can help one another find your higher wisdom in all the hard moments and funny bits and sad times that happen to all of us. It is easier to get to the heart of the matter and walk with your biggest fears and feelings when there are others there, ready to listen, step-for-step beside you.

But know that none of this is a given. Open hearts, open doors and like minds are a rare gift. Sometimes, acquaintances turn into companions and companions become friends, but not every time. If you are lucky enough to

find it, true friendship will fill the spaces in your soul like nothing else. A real friendship will enrich and illuminate your life. You will be seen and heard in an exquisite exchange of mutual validation and support that builds a deep trust like no other.

If they are already there for you, cherish them, these true friends of yours. If not, take the first step. Be courageous and risk your heart. Be yourself, above all else. Strive to be the friend you want to have and you may find yourself with a community for life.

Shvaygert Ekaterina/Shutterstock.com

Be gentle
with yourself.

*Try not to confuse
how you are feeling
with how you are doing.*

Dear new mom:

Becoming a mom is powerful. It is a dynamic, moment-to-moment experience that brings dimension to your life that you could never otherwise imagine. Your love multiplies; your feelings like fear and frustration intensify; and your vulnerability can bring you to tears.

Emotions run high from the time you decide that you want to become a mother. But in a moment, they can shift and change. Hold a place inside for all your feelings – they have purpose and they will teach you. There are times when you will feel so alone. Reach out and reach in for comfort. And there will be times when your emotions overwhelm you. Feel them, honour them and use them – they will give you important information. Then share them, especially with the understanding and compassionate souls in your midst.

I have witnessed many a mother's warrior heart, fierce and strong. I have witnessed selflessness, helplessness, terror and fatigue. Your willingness to be a mom is big. You ask over and over, "Am I up to this?" No matter. You will do it anyway.

Know that the simple acts of everyday life are everything to your child. Remember that your struggles in no way overshadow the biggest truth: your child is lucky to have you as a mother. You are an ever-present witness to his unique life.

But with all the giving, don't forget yourself. There must be a balance. The greatest gift you can give your child is a mother who has care and compassion for herself. Put your baby into the care of someone trusted, and do whatever you need to do to reunite with yourself. Return refreshed and ready to be the loving and responsive mother that you are.

Believe in your capacity to live a life of happiness. Practise feeling gratitude for each moment. Dare to be joyful. When you find yourself racing, slow yourself to live in the moment.

There will be rewards. There will come a time when you look at your adult children and be moved to tears just because of their very existence. They are alive because of you – and you were there every step of the way. You will be in awe of the miracle of life and the cycle of things. You will become incredibly grateful just to have been a participant.

You made this leap of faith. Your feminine energy and all your other energies are supporting life. You have my deepest respect. You are a hero.

Anne Peace

Part 3: Other Mothers

Whether it was last month or 30 years ago, the first days of a child's life leave an imprint like no other on a mother's soul. These stories, shared by women about early motherhood, offer comfort and wisdom to other mothers.

Enjoy.

Claire

Submitted by Claire Plivcic

All three of my babies' births (and their first years) were very different. Initially, I thought that was because my children are very different personalities, but with hindsight I think it was because I was a very different person each time. Each child has left a very definite footprint on my personality and the way I view the world. It's funny really, because we think that as parents we are the instructors and the ones who are supposed to leave a change in the way our children view the world, when actual fact it is quite the reverse.

The birth of my first child made me feel like the strongest woman on Earth. Just after he was born, I felt so connected to both him and my husband. I felt we had the whole parenting thing sorted. I was therefore totally blindsided by how crippling I would find the ridiculously high expectations that I held myself to. Leo was actually a relatively easygoing baby, but the need to do things perfectly and feeling like I was always failing to be the mother and wife I thought I should be were very isolating. It wasn't until I made the effort to get out and meet other mothers, when Leo was nearly 10 months old, that I realized there were a lot more mothers like me.

My second child's birth was more about survival than empowerment. I'll never really forget how scared I felt the hour before she made her arrival into the world. But if

Trinacria Photo/Shutterstock.com

> But if Eleanor's birth was traumatic, her first six months brought both me and my husband to our knees. She... just cried all the time.

Eleanor's birth was traumatic, her first six months brought both me and my husband to our knees (literally!). She was a baby who just cried all the time. But what amazes me about that time was how strongly I felt about her. By all reason, I should have truly disliked this little being who had entered our lives like a hurricane and seemed intent on destroying any moment of peace we could find, but in actual fact I was fiercely protective of her. Somehow the intensity of her emotions brought out the same in me.

My third child's birth was a gift. There is no other way to explain what I think was one of the most perfect experiences I have ever had. I didn't fight the pain or analyze what was happening. I was just in the moment. Unlike my other births, I didn't feel the need to have my husband next to me every second. I just knew that I could do this, it was me and my baby and

Jill

Submitted by Jill Snidal

My baby had arrived, and my feelings were a blend of awe, fear and anticipation. Nothing that I heard in prenatal classes prepared me for how I felt at this moment. In the safety net of the hospital room, I embraced my new child, my hemorrhoids and my husband.

Once we arrived home, I waited for those natural instincts and my milk to arrive. The milk came sooner, along with sore nipples and fatigue. Ah motherhood...as honey is to bees – not in my neighbourhood!

Motherhood is a new destination, but there are no tour guides. This is a place where there are no routines, no schedules – and very likely experiences and emotions that you may not have imagined you would ever experience:

sadness, fear, joy, love, guilt, and the protectiveness of a mother bear.

This destination will demand that you accept yourself and your partner with all your strengths and limitations, in living colour. This will be a time in your life where you will soar and stumble, but that's OK. Every day, you will need to look in the mirror and tell yourself that you are OK. Because it is OK to curse and cry, love and be loved, ask for and accept help.

This is a destination that you cannot alter. There is no option to change travel plans. As you wipe away the tears of joy and sadness, this will be the most incredible journey in your lifetime. •

we were going to be OK. Marilla has always been a very easy-to-love baby. She definitely presents challenges, like any child. But somehow the feeling I had during her birth has never really left us. She, more than either of my other children, seems to have a way of looking at me that reminds me to enjoy the moment and just be. •

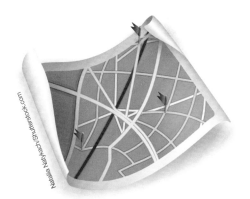

Pat

Submitted by Pat Roberts

It's a bit unsettling to admit this. My memories of my two sons' first years are very vague. There are not many sharp images from those months that pop into my mind, almost 30 and 25 years ago respectively, unless prompted by a photograph (of which there are many, thank goodness) or the reminiscences of others who shared our world.

There were no extreme or unusual conditions that created this brain fog. In fact, I expect that there are quite a few others like me, who spent much of the time just doing the

> Being a new mom left me exhilarated, blissful, painfully exhausted, and full of wonder and awe. I felt completely powerful, yet woefully inadequate.

best I could on very little sleep and without much assistance. My husband was a police officer who worked shifts and was also permanently on call for a special division of his police department, so I was on my own quite often.

The reality of being a new mom left me exhilarated, blissful, painfully exhausted, and full of wonder and awe. I felt completely powerful, yet woefully inadequate. Sleep deprivation will bring the strongest of us to our knees. It seemed, especially in those early days, that I gave and gave and gave everything of myself to this tiny being that required me to find a way to give even more. How could I possibly have anything more to give to such a demanding little creature?

Then, one day, it happened. Around six weeks of age, my precious son looked deep into my eyes and smiled a big, goofy, gummy smile. On purpose! I made him HAPPY. And in that moment, I knew everything up to that point, and from that point on, was absolutely worth it.

No matter how fuzzy my memories are about much of their first years, my sons' first smiles are indelibly imprinted in my mind forever. •

Elizabeth

Submitted by Elizabeth Wickerman

A chance encounter in a grocery store taught me that even mothers need reassurance and recognition.

It happened at the grocery store. I was with my baby daughter. She was six or seven months old at the time. I had just settled her into the seat of the cart when an older gentleman approached, smiling at my baby. We chatted for a moment, then he said, "This little girl looks like she is very well cared for. You are doing a very good job with her." As he turned to go on his way, I felt the emotion rise from deep in my stomach. To my surprise, I very nearly burst into tears in the middle of the produce department.

His words seemed to fit into an empty space in my heart that I didn't know was there. I knew I wanted so very badly to be a good mother to my daughter. I didn't know how badly I needed to hear it. People were quick to give me all kinds of parenting advice, but it seemed that simple positive feedback was in short supply. And I didn't want to ask – I feared that any need for reassurance would put me squarely in the "bad mother" category. Wasn't I supposed to take to motherhood naturally and easily, and weren't the inherent rewards of baby care supposed to be enough? I wasn't looking for a trophy – I guess I just needed to know for sure that I really was doing a good job raising my baby girl.

That day, a kind gentleman reminded me that my needs still counted, and that I indeed was succeeding. It was the very first time anyone ever told me, unequivocally, that I was a good mother.

And it was exactly the thing I needed to hear. •

Eva

Submitted by Eva Martinez

The day my daughter was born, I was so caught up in the excitement and anticipation that I didn't even stop to think that things might not go smoothly. Three days past my due date, I thought I was ready. After all, I had already stopped working, and it was frustrating to be on maternity leave without a baby to care for! After 26 hours of labour, she

> We...had acquired all the equipment, but we completely underestimated how much our lives would be changed by a baby.

was born, but with the umbilical cord wrapped around her neck twice there were significant complications. I did not get to hold her for over four hours, after she was taken away by the respiratory team.

The first six weeks of her life were a challenge. On one hand, it was absolutely amazing to hold her and watch her. I never wanted to let her go, and I hated to have to put her down. It was hard to believe that my husband and I had created something so beautiful, and the love I felt for her was overwhelming.

But between the postpartum hormonal roller coaster, troubles with breastfeeding, and the sheer exhaustion of sleep-deprived days and nights, at times I felt that I was simply unprepared for motherhood. Yes, we had done the prenatal courses, prepared a beautiful nursery and acquired all the supplies and equipment. But we completely underestimated how much our lives would be changed by a baby.

Fortunately everything got better with time. So much so that I recently gave birth to our third child. Motherhood is a much more comfortable role now. With this birth, I'm the most relaxed I've ever been.

With breastfeeding, I've since come to accept (and I share this revelation with new mothers when I can) that it's a learned process, unique to each child, and that it's

definitely not as natural as I was led to believe. Motherhood has made me better – although not yet perfect – at asking for help, and I am very appreciative of those on whom I can count. I still struggle with wanting to do it all myself – a trait that challenges me in my personal and professional relationships.

Motherhood has also revealed a lot of ugly truths about the very toxic relationship I have with my own mother and the importance of making sure I do not make the same mistakes she made. •

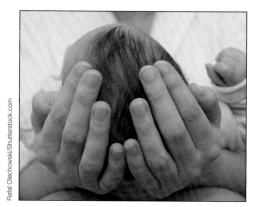

Rafal Olechowski/Shutterstock.com

Photos courtesy of the Gilbert-Sheppard family

Jenny

Submitted by Jenny Gilbert

The moment Veronica was placed on my chest, I felt a sense of accomplishment and intense pride – in myself and in my baby. Natural childbirth was the most painful experience of my life – I could never have known how difficult it would be – but it was also the most incredibly rewarding and exhilarating. I see now why reading birth stories and watching videos could never have prepared me for that moment – the realization that this little, squawking human being was made and nurtured by my body. It really does feel like I am the first person on Earth to have this experience.

The days after giving birth had me feeling totally elated. "I did this!," I thought. While I felt extreme exhaustion caring for her, especially in those first few days as my body was recovering, I have never felt happier or more content with my life. Truthfully, I expected it to be harder and less satisfying. After a difficult pregnancy, I worried that parenting would be, frankly, as disappointing as pregnancy had been.

I feel lucky and grateful that I am enjoying this time so much because I can already feel how quickly it is passing by. I feel proud and relieved when I make it through each night, because nighttime is hard and can feel so isolating. I feel such pride in my body nourishing hers.

I never knew I could experience emotions this intense or feel this vulnerable. Watching her sleep, I feel amazement and love. I also feel protective and fear for her life. I feel such wonder at the fact that she's been in my life a short time. It truly feels like we are meant to be together. •

Your story

....

....

....

....

....

....

....

....

....

....

....

....

....

....

References and further reading

Beck, M. (2003). *The Joy Diet: 10 Practices for a Happier Life*. New York: Crown Publishers.

Ben-Shahar, T. (2007). *Happier: Learn the Secrets to Daily Joy and Lasting Fulfillment*. New York: McGraw-Hill.

_____. (2009). *The Pursuit of Perfect: How to Stop Chasing Perfection and Start Living a Richer, Happier Life*. New York: McGraw-Hill.

Branden, N. (1994). *Six Pillars of Self-Esteem*. New York: Bantam Books.

Brown, B. (2007). *I Thought It Was Just Me (but it isn't): Telling the Truth About Perfectionism, Inadequacy and Power*. New York: Penguin/Gotham Books.

_____. (2010). *The Gifts of Imperfection: Let Go of Who You Think You're Supposed to Be and Embrace Who You Are*. Center City: Hazelden.

Carey, W.B., M.D. (2004). *Understanding Your Child's Temperament*. The Children's Hospital of Philadelphia: Replica Books.

Csikszentmihalyi, M. (1990). *Flow: The Psychology of Optimal Experience*. New York: Harper Collins.

Dalai Lama and Cutler, H. (1998). *The Art of Happiness: A Handbook for Living*. New York: Riverhead.

Emmons, R. (2007). *Thanks: How the New Science of Gratitude Can Make You Happier*. New York: Houghton Mifflin.

Fredrickson, B. (2009). *Positivity*. New York: Crown Publishers.

Gilbert, D. (2005). *Stumbling on Happiness*. New York: Vintage Books.

Hanh, T.N. (1996). *The Long Road Turns to Joy: A Guide to Walking Meditation*. Berkeley: Parallax.

Holden, R. (1998). *Happiness Now!* London: Coronet Books.

Lyubomirsky, S. (2008). *The How of Happiness*. New York: Penguin.

Peck, M.S. (1978). *The Road Less Traveled: A New Psychology of Love, Traditional Values and Spiritual Growth*. New York: Simon & Schuster.

Seligman, M.E.P. (2002). *Authentic Happiness: Using the New Positive Psychology to Realize Your Potential for Lasting Fulfillment*. New York: Free Press.

_____. (1991). *Learned Optimism: How to Change Your Mind and Your Life*. New York: Knopf.

_____. (1995). *The Optimistic Child*. Boston: Houghton Mifflin.

Tieger, Paul D. and Barron-Tieger, Barbara (1997). *Nurture by Nature: Understand Your Child's Personality Type — and Become a Better Parent*. New York: Little, Brown and Company.